Mel B
BLUES HARP CLASS
Favorite Blues Solo

Table Of

Harmonica Notation 2
San Francisco Bay Blues 4
Beale Street Blues 12
Frankie & Johnny 20
Alabama Bound 21
Wanderin' 25
Deep River Blues 28

1 2 3 4 5 6 7 8 9 0

© 1997 BY MEL BAY PUBLICATIONS, INC., PACIFIC, MO 63069.
ALL RIGHTS RESERVED. INTERNATIONAL COPYRIGHT SECURED. B.M.I.
MADE AND PRINTED IN U.S.A.
Visit us on the Web at www.melbay.com • E-mail us at email@melbay.com

Harmonica Tablature

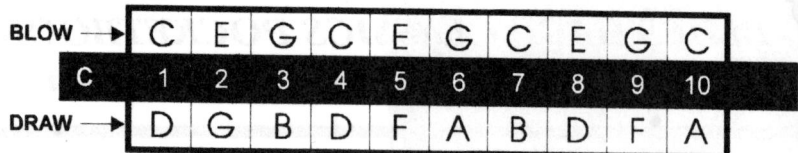

A number is placed under the notational symbol that corresponds to the hole that is to be played. When a note stands by itself, the note is to be drawn upon (inhaled). When a note is proceeded with a plus (+), the note is to be blown (exhaled). If the note is to be bent, a series of slashes will be notated to the right of the hole. Each slash represents a half-step bend. For example: three draw (3), bent down a half-step, would be "B-flat" and would be notated as 3'. Three draw, bent down a whole-step, would be "A" and would be notated as 3". Three draw, bent down a whole-step and one-half (minor third bend), would be "A-flat" and would be notated as 3'''. Diagrammed below is the entire bend chart for a "C" major diatonic harmonica.

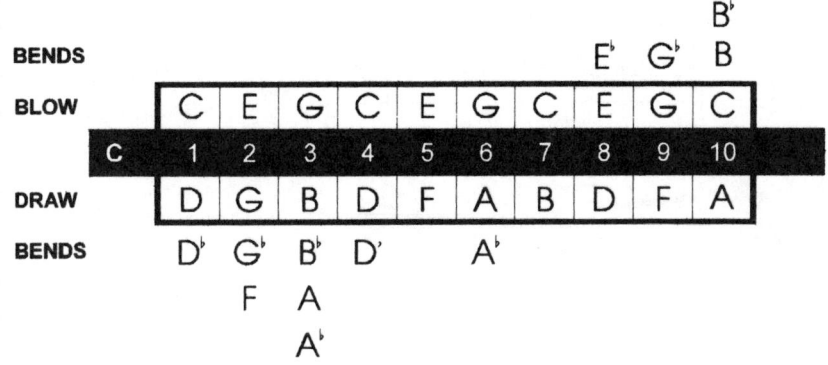

Beale Street Blues

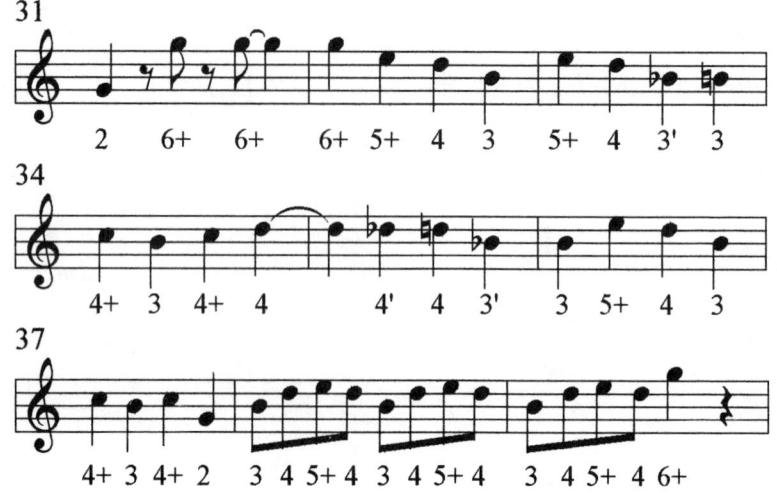

Alabama Bound

27

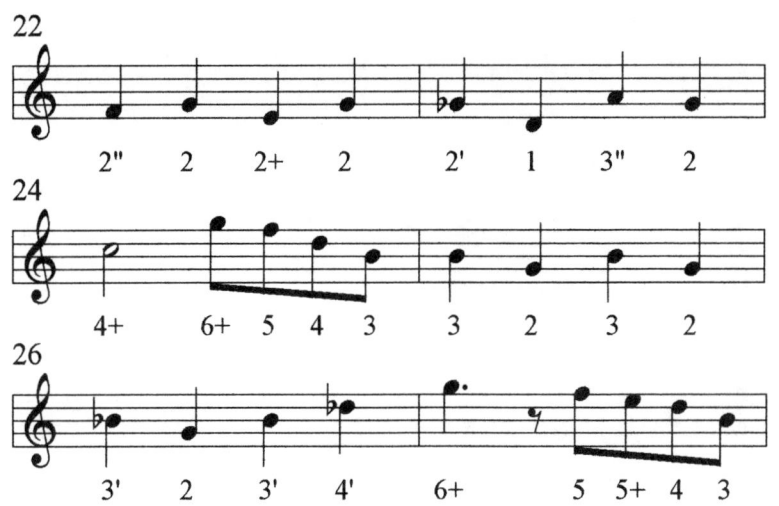